I0504404

Airbnb careers

How to Invest in Airbnb at Zero Cost

How to Improve the Rate of Return on Investment of Airbnb

How to Make Airbnb Automation Management

Table of Contents

Preface Investment Opportunities

Chapter 1 One My First Barrel of Gold

1 This is my story

2 Advantages of Airbnb

3 Location of Airbnb

4 Importance of rental contract

Chapter 2 Notices for Airbnb

1 Airbnb Security

2 Response to the poor review

3 Title and main pictures

Chapter 3 Improvement of Airbnb's Return on Investment

1 Soft loading skills

2. Increase the added value of Airbnb

3. How to invest in Airbnb at zero cost

4. Is Airbnb's decoration expensive?

5 Airbnb Automation Management

Preface

In recent years, with the escalation of consumption, China's tourism consumption has repeatedly set a new record. With the vigorous development of tourism, a new way of accommodation - airbnb has emerged. This new way has been people's consumption enthusiasm and favor, and I also accompanied by this opportunity to earn the first barrel of gold in life. Looking at the trend, standing in the right team, making money is naturally easy, I also hope to share some experience and experience to you, hope that eventually everyone can achieve financial freedom.

Chapter 1 One My First Barrel of Gold

1 This is my story

2 Advantages of Airbnb

3 Location of Airbnb

4 Importance of rental contract

Property may serve you, but it may enslave you.

This is my story.

I used to be an ordinary college graduate, a professional engineer. Every day, my job was to calculate the engineering quantities. There are more and more drawings on the table. I felt that there would never be an end. I lived a boring and boring life every day.   However, with the passage of time, so seven years later, to see that the balance of accounts is always a balance of payments, never extra money to invest, nor dare to buy some luxury goods, monthly wages deduct mortgages, car maintenance, and living expenses. There was hardly any money at all. The family had surgery because of illness, spent the remaining balance, and the wife's business failure made it worse. The account changed from zero to negative, but the salary I earned from work was not enough to make up for the hole. It was the idea of resigning and starting a business that started to create one. It belongs to my own business.

But at the beginning, the family was strongly against it, because if I quit my job, I would face a further increase in the account deficit, because salary is my only source of income, I like freedom, but with the pressure of life, gradually lost freedom, swallowed up by the pressure of life. I am totally lost in my work. My time belongs to my boss. I feel like a prisoner in prison. I'll be locked in at 9 a.m. and released at 5 p.m. Of course, the time of work will depend on the mood of my boss. Delaying work is a common practice. Sometimes I always think about it. Is it because I don't work hard? Why is the account balance getting smaller and smaller? What is it that eats away my money? I have seen the old engineers who have worked together for more than 20 years. Their salaries are only a little higher than ours, and they are so old that they have to do such heavy work. After retirement, retired workers in many countries in the world still have to find a job to continue working until they are physically unable to work, and most importantly, they can't. The result is that the money did not earn much, the body collapsed, with the money to treat their own physical diseases, which is a very sad thing, but also 80% of the people will take a road, it is obvious that I will not take such a road.

Some people will come up with many ways to start a business, but they are not willing to take the first step, always hesitant. Ultimately, you have to go back to work day after day. Parents and friends generally have not done business, their first reaction is that there are risks in doing business, but the second half of the sentence will only be understood if you do it yourself, that is, risk is controllable, as the teacher always said at school: genius is 99% of the sweat and 1% of the inspiration, so hard work is very important. But the second half is that, but sometimes that one percent of the inspiration is more important than that ninety-nine percent of the sweat. Entrepreneurship is not only risk-free but also stable compared with work. Later, I happened to see Airbnb on the Internet. Before investing in this industry, I also made a full data analysis. Where to choose rooms, where the flow of passengers is relatively large, and the surrounding traffic is convenient, so I chose a house next to the scenic spot. The advantage of the scenic spot room is that the flow of passengers is large and the price of the house is easy to accept. Return on investment is high, there are guests in the offseason and in the peak season. From room selection-decoration-operation, a complete set of experiences, let me realize what the real market is. Business is not really such a difficult thing as parents and friends say. In the process, a lot of risk control measures have been taken, which has increased my ability to control risks. Plus hired cleaners, forming an automated operation system, and ultimately achieved passive income, let me lie at home watching TV, you can easily make money. This is the first time that I feel the charm of passive income.

In China, the current situation of real estate is well known, domestic rent return rate within the scope of China, the rate of return is declining. The reason is that the rate of house price rise is much higher than that of rent. According to the research data, from 2004 to 2008, the rate of house price increase in China is as high as 60% to 100%, while the rate of rent increase is only about 2%. Shanghai has deviated from this value for a long time, and if it is in accordance with international standards, the current housing prices in Shanghai are more than twice the reasonable price. Investing in residential housing is one of the effective measures to improve real estate returns. I have always believed in the concept of cash flow. Only investment with positive cash flow is really a good investment. For ordinary people, if you don't have enough money to invest in real estate, it's a good start to do business to be a second landlord. With the increase in income, you can expand your business next year. A house turns into a second house and a second house into four houses, which has a compound interest effect.

Advantages of Airbnb

Airbnb has become a fashionable thing both abroad and at home, but why do some people choose it? How is it different from a hotel?

Advantage 1: Curiosity about new things

Compared with hotels, residential accommodation is a new thing. People feel fresh and curious. The hostel is rich in functions and built with local customs and customs. It not only has basic accommodation functions but also has great ornamental value. Moreover, the accommodation is suitable for many people to stay together, to travel and live, to travel collectively and to travel. To be honest, Airbnb is generally cheaper than traditional hotels, especially when the number of people is more than three.

Advantage 2: Diversified style of accommodation

Airbnb decoration style has little repeatability, each has its own personality and theme, which will not cause aesthetic fatigue. Landlords have different themes and orientations for Airbnb, some of which are cold and strong design style, some of which are warm and grounded feelings, and some of which have the significance of inheritance -- -- -- -- -- -- -- -- There's always an Airbnb house, and you'll be interested in staying.

1. Landscape-enjoying and vacation-type accommodation

The combination of natural landscape or carefully planned artificial landscapes, such as the night scene of 10,000 lights, stars in the sky, garden landscape, grassland flowers or alpine sea, etc.

2. Art Experience Airbnb

Tourists are led by operators to experience various art production activities, including pottery kneading, sculpture, painting, clogs, jelly candles, sky lantern making, etc. Tourists can personally create artworks and experience rural or modern art and culture feasts.

3.Rural experience Airbnb

In the traditional agricultural countryside, besides providing rural landscape and experiencing farm life, there are also experiential activities in agricultural production, supporting sightseeing orchards, vegetable gardens, and tea gardens。

Living in the countryside for a few days, let your body feel comfortable and happy, enjoy the life of roaming food and roaming, whether North or south, can be convenient and comfortable, this journey is an idyllic journey, a spiritual journey, but also an unforgettable holiday.

4. Hot Spring Residence

Exquisite Hot Spring Suite equipment, each suite has its own characteristics, generous and enlarged soup pool and equipped with SPA, massage, cold and hot pool equipment.

Hot spring lodging is like feeling at home, relax heartily and let nature be the best medical doctor.

5. Retro Airbnb

Its accommodation environment is renovated by the design blueprint of the style of ancient buildings, providing visitors with deep nostalgic experience.

Advantage 3: Feelings

More importantly, there is one more attractive element in the Airbnb than in the hotel, that is, feelings. The way of life and life experience of the Airbnb is a major selling point of Airbnb.

Most of the hosts are idealists and perfectionists. They try their best to make the accommodation perfect and share it with you. In a sense, the people who run houses are all artists. Visitors prefer to live in Airbnb, in fact, they live in the deep and shallow feelings of the host people.

Site Selection of Residence

Among many kinds of residential accommodation, I choose to do is this kind of urban residential accommodation, because the investment is small and the return is large, the flow of people is stable, coupled with previous experience as a construction engineer, more familiar with house decoration.

1. Determine the size of the Airbnb

Before correctly choosing the size and location of residential accommodation, operators must determine the size of residential accommodation. Because it is only after the size of the accommodation is determined that it is possible to find the right housing in the right location.

2 Site Selection Criteria

(1)The selection criteria of geographical location.

The standard show for choosing accommodation requires a clean and sanitary environment, clean air and no noise pollution. It's better to have better greening and beautiful buildings around.

(2) Economic selection criteria

The economic characteristics of the residential environment directly affect the operation of residential quarters, and corresponding countermeasures must be made according to their characteristics. For example, different marketing strategies should be adopted for residential accommodation in business, business, industrial, university, entertainment or residential areas with different characteristics, as well as their different scales and grades. We should pay attention to the economic development trend of the selected area, especially the speed of commercial development. These factors have a great impact on the future of restaurants.

(3) Market selection criteria

The competitiveness of the same type of accommodation in the region will largely affect future profits.

(4) Consider the source of passengers

It is better to choose both residential areas and commercial areas.

3 Typical residential areas

(1) Near important stations

Near the station, there are many customers, including travelers, businessmen, students and so on. For different customers, the way of

Airbnb service should be different, especially the pricing problem should be handled carefully.

(2) Holiday Concentrated Areas
White-collar workers and business people who work in the company are the main customers of Airbnb. Most of their visits are for business or vacation purposes. These customers generally have higher consumption and pay more attention to the grade, decoration and service quality of residential accommodation. If managed properly, it will bring you a lot of profits.

(3) Student street

(4) Business Downtown

(5)Various types of residential areas
Customers in this area are mainly residents in the vicinity of the residential area. The focus of hospitality is how to show warmth and provide fresh and delicious catering.

(6)Suburban section

(7) Large Hospital
Some patients with major diseases and their families need long-term treatment in a hospital. The patient can live in a hospital, but his family must need accommodation.
If your house is next to a very famous local or even domestic hospital, that's a good choice.

(8)Near School
First, couples with weekend needs.
Secondly, every year, many foreign students come to China from abroad to study. The learning cycle is usually 1-3 months.

(9)Near the net red shop.

You can often see the recommendation of a certain net red shop, a restaurant, a certain milk tea shop, the queue is crowded every day. If you have five net red shops downstairs, there will be many people coming to live in your house. Because young people now socialize through the Internet, it is very attractive for young people to recommend things on the Internet.

Importance of rental contract

1. In the rental contract, we must clearly and clearly tell the landlord what the house is for. If you don't tell the landlord, The landlord will take back your house

2. Airbnb is often renovated, requiring additional investment from landlords. If you sign a one-year contract for too short a period of time, all your efforts in the next year will be in vain.

3. When signing a rental contract, we must write out the landlord's liability for breach of contract. If he take back the house in advance, how much will he need to compensate for it?

4. Tomorrow there are many unknowns, I suggest making an appointment with the landlord. If you don't want to rent within the contract period, you can sublet the house or transfer your rental contract.

5. After determining the rent, the tenant can strive for more than half a month from the landlord to renovate the house and tidy up the house.

Chapter 2 Notices for Airbnb

1 Airbnb Security

2 Response to the poor review

3 Title and main pictures

Airbnb Safety

Foundation Safety

1. Ask in advance if the occupant has any elderly or children, and remind the guests to pay attention to relevant safety matters, such as windows, balconies, stairs, etc.

2. Install or prepare fire extinguishers, smoke alarms, medical first aid kits, sound control lights, flashlights, and other escape tools. Explain the location of such safety facilities to guests when they check-in, and give them the most comprehensive and timely personal and property safety protection measures.

3. Develop housing safety manual, provide landlord emergency contact telephone, surrounding hospital, police station location and telephone, and other information needed by tenants in an emergency, and put safety manual in a prominent position.

4. Detection is the first step to prevention. Do a good job of testing regularly, and ensure that safety information is updated in the description of housing sources.

Kitchen safety

The kitchen is the "disaster area" that involves many dangerous factors.

1. Gas inspection: Regular inspection of gas pipelines and valves to prevent gas leakage, can be posted above the gas stove "Guidelines for the safe use of gas".

2. Fire extinguishing device: The kitchen should be equipped with a smoke sense and sprinkler device. The device has no shield, and the test is effective. If there is no such device, the fire extinguisher can be placed.

3. Food safety: kitchens should try not to provide food materials and condiments, so as to avoid food safety disputes and other issues.

4. Regular ventilation: install ventilation devices; open windows frequently to maintain air fluidity.

5. Keep away from combustibles: Do not place combustibles near the stove, such as oil, alcohol, plastic products, etc.

Bathroom safety

1. Explosion-proof: Glass shower room, must stick explosion-proof film, otherwise the broken glass bursts everywhere and splashes to the guests, the consequences are very serious.

2. Anti-skid: dry and wet separation, keep the site dry outside the bath; anti-skid building materials for the ground; anti-skid mats for the bathroom.

3. Anti-electricity: There are sockets in the bathroom. Keep away from the water source and cover them to reduce the risk factor of leakage.

4. Handrail: The bathroom can be equipped with an additional safety handrail, not only to care for the elderly and children but also as a shelf to receive shower gel, shampoo, and other supplies.

Electricity safety

1. Select qualified household appliances, and regularly check and maintain the normal operation of electrical equipment in the house.

2. Regular inspection of wiring, switches, plugs, sockets and other accessories, timely maintenance or replacement if problems are found.

3. Make instructions for the use of electrical appliances, place the instructions in a prominent position, and remind tenants to read them carefully.

Public safety

1. Balcony: Balcony guardrail should be attached with safety tips. When the height of the balcony guardrail is less than 135 cm, it is necessary to install a protective net.

2. Entry: Make sure that the building ban, access control, door lock, elevator, window and so on are in good condition.

3. Passage: Ensure the fire passage is unobstructed, avoid accumulating inflammable debris and post-emergency evacuation sketch.

Response to the poor review

Word of mouth is the most important thing in the management of Airbnb quarters. A good evaluation will motivate guests. But bad reviews are not necessarily bad things, and they can also play a role. As long as there are affirmation and praise of the Airbnb in the evaluation, it will also have a fair foresight and measurement of other potential guests. If encounter malicious bad reviews, landlords should think about how to respond to such a bad review, so as to make timely remedies and minimize losses. You know, the process of comment and reply is the process of product re-exposure, and the opportunity to show your accommodation!

I. Complaint Hardware Facility Class Differential Evaluation

Customers complain about the hardware of the equipment, such as air conditioning, hot water, lighting, etc. The landlord's friends must regularly repair the hardware facilities in the house and don't delay when they find that the equipment is in trouble, so as not to give a big bad review to the guests.

But there are remedies if the guest gives a bad comment.
1. Solve problems in time and repair equipment.
2. In the comments, thank the tenants for their help in pointing out the problems and indicating that the problems have been solved. Welcome the guests to check in again.

II. Health Differential Assessment
Health is the most important and intolerable problem for tenants. If the landlord does not pay attention to household hygiene, he will not only get bad reviews but also make a lot of effort to go down the drain.
How to respond to poor health assessment?
1. Expressing apologies and explaining reasonably
2. Indicate that the problem has been solved
3. Strengthen the management of follow-up health services

III Complaint Geographical Position Difference Assessment
1.Directions for different groups of people.
Men are particularly sensitive to the orientation of the southeast and Northwest。
Women are more likely to identify with the way they perceive the road from front to back.

2. Find out the characteristic buildings or larger brands near the residential quarters, and use these landmarks to guide the tenants.

3. Draw an interesting simplified version of the road map and upload it to the platform or place it in the room for the tenant's reference.

IV. Complaints about Housing Types and Charges

1. Highlighting Other Highlights of Residence

2. Emphasize the quality of oneself and the cost of design and decoration

3. It can express the degree of the devotion of some homeowners to their houses.

Title and main pictures

1 Understanding Platform Retrieval Mechanism

According to the double search mechanism of the location and title of the room source, we recommend the room source for the tenants. Therefore, it is very important to include important landmarks near your house source in the title of the house source.

2. Understanding Tenant Search Habits

In the process of searching the source of rooms, the most searched are landmarks, apartment types, and styles. Landmark is an important landmark near the house mentioned in the first point. Household type is the source type, such as one room, one hall, independent single room, three rooms with a large balcony and other descriptions. Style is the decoration style of the house or suitable living scene, such as Nordic style, small and fresh, lover's room, peripheral tour, etc. If your title carries a style description and meets our label adding rules, it will be added to the system with corresponding labels, which will help to improve the ranking of housing sources.

3 Titles Prioritize the Display of Important Information

Therefore, it is particularly important to put important information in front. There are some more literary headlines, which look very poetic but do not reveal important information.

4 Headings should have identifiable information

If the house type and decoration style are similar, the title of the house source will be silly and unclear. Therefore, adding identifiable information in the title can directly locate the source of the house when the tenant consults, so as to facilitate the landlord to view the status of the source.

Chapter 3   Improvement of Airbnb's Return on Investment

1 Soft loading skills
2. Increase the added value of Airbnb
3. How to invest in Airbnb at zero cost
4. Is Airbnb's decoration expensive?
5 Airbnb Automation Management

Rich people never want to miss an opportunity to show off their vulgarity.

How to match the soft loading design?

1. The premise of practical function: In the home environment, the function must be greater than the appreciation, so the design of home soft-fitting should play a practical and reasonable basis. For example, when choosing furniture, lamps, ornaments and so on, we should pay attention to the space function and match it on the basis of space demand, so as to achieve the integration of function and layout and balance space design.

2. Style and style should be the same: the decoration of indoor soft clothing should be unified in style, such as fabric soft clothing, lighting design, tone matching, etc., all around the unifying principle. In the interior design, while guaranteeing to meet every preference, there are some things that seek common ground while reserving differences.

3. Space tone should be balanced: Color collocation is very important in the design of home software because the color is very intuitive and visible. It follows the law of color, knows how to change in the same place, and takes into account both contrast and fusion, which can also increase the overall complementary.

Key Points of Soft Assembly Design

01

Furniture

A large category of soft-fitting is all the furniture in the house, which can be divided into sofas, tables and chairs, wardrobes and so on. It is an indispensable part of the decoration. When choosing furniture, we must choose to accord with the theme style of the home.

02 cloth art

Another indispensable is cloth art, which plays the role of decoration. If furniture is the skeleton of the whole house, cloth art should be regarded as the soul of soft clothing. Cloth art can be roughly divided into pillows, curtains, bedding, carpets, tablecloths and so on.

03 Green Flower Planting

Green flower planting should be an indispensable soft outfit for every house. It has both practicability and beauty. Green planting, while purifying the air, becomes the unique landscape of the whole family with its unique green meaning.

What is the advantage of soft-fitting is that it is flexible and plasticity, so it is easy to adjust. It's not the same. There is no good-looking or bad-looking soft clothing, the key is to see whether the design is suitable for oneself and whether it is consistent with the whole home design style. Good furnishings will maximize the expression of decorations, highlighting the overall style of the room design.

Attention to details:

There are large full-body mirrors near the hanger.

Whether guests can easily find a night light when they get up at night?

Is there clothes rack for towels and clothes in the bathroom?

If the target object is a family, it provides enough space for children to move around, and the corner of the desk and chair is protected.

Simple medicine box (common cold medicine, carsickness medicine, gastrointestinal medicine, bandage, etc.)

If you are in a tourist city, a few pages of travel strategy/map is also a good choice.

Increase the added value of Airbnb accommodation

Apart from providing accommodation, what additional sources of income do Airbnb provide? Here's an introduction to providing additional services. The landlord can provide some services, including shuttle flights, scenic spots, food strategies and so on; furthermore, he can arrange rooms for the tenants (marriage room
party room); he can also provide local folk services, such as taking the tenants fishing, preparing seafood meals for the guests, and taking them to the sea. Participate in local festivals or entertainment programs, etc. Provide resources. The landlord can provide some low-cost scenic spot tickets, low-cost tour groups, the introduction of charter service, the recommendation of local fine local products and so on.

I. Commercial shooting/theater rental

Crowds of audiences: theater crew / Taobao sellers/internet stars

Profit Point: Additional Commercial Filming Fee

There are some very literary and artistic residences designed with style, so they will be selected as commercial shooting base by some netizens. In addition, film and television crews sometimes have some indoor shooting needs, they will rent houses for shooting.

II Marriage premises/party premises , etc.

Audience: Newlyweds/Birthday Crowds Profit Point: Additional Fees for Marriage Room Arrangement and Wedding Planning

Nowadays, many newly married couples do not like the uniform pattern of hotels. They prefer to hold their own wedding in such a warm and distinctive place as residential quarters.

III Characteristic Theme Room: party Room/Competition Room/Cartoon characters Theme/Disney Theme, etc.
Audience group: For the faithful enthusiasts of electronic competition/quadratic or an element, profit points: charging for boarding fees and selling snacks, etc. (Take electronic competition room as an example) Electric Competition Room: Most of them are suitable for men. They have shelf beds and don't need much rest.

To meet the diverse needs of the population, the functions of residential accommodation are also varied. Often, due to economic ability or some reasons, it is impossible to decorate their family into a special feature that they like, so living in residential quarters has become a kind of sustenance for these people to realize their deep desire.。

IV. RV/Tent/Snow House/Wooden House/Boat House/planet House/etc.

Audience group: people who want to experience different accommodation needs are profitable points: to enhance the added value of Airbnb in addition to accommodation

The characteristic housing types such as wooden houses, vacation villas, courtyards, duplex Loft, tents, caves and so on, undoubtedly meet the psychological needs of tourists in pursuit of novelty and novelty.

If your hotel is near the snow mountain, you can take your guest's skiing. In the seaside accommodation, you can take the tenants out to sea for fishing. These are combined with the customs and customs of the place where the accommodation is located to achieve additional profits.

V Cooperate with scenic spots to sell tickets to the public: Profit points

for those who specialize in traveling: Ticket sharing

Residence in the vicinity of the scenic area, you can talk about some cooperation with the scenic area. Tickets can be sold to tenants at a price lower than some OTA ticket purchasing pipelines. In this way, the landlord can increase some revenue from ticket sales.

VI. Emotional training places (zither, tea ceremony, flower way, etc.)

Audience group: the profit point of the person who is eager for knowledge: setting up a training place in his own residence, charging a training fee

VII. Seascape House and Home-lodging near Scenic Spot

Audience group: The profit point of the traveling group is to attract customers in by selling seascape, river view and so on. Prices have increased considerably in peak season.

Hostels with selling points can at least rise a lot in price compared with those in the same neighborhood. If marketing is well done, many people can be attracted to punch in and take pictures, even if not for accommodation.

How to invest in Airbnb at zero cost

Some people think that any investment needs money, even a lot of money. In fact, the real investment is not like this, but needs the right opportunity, because experience and opportunity are more valuable than money. When you invest more, you will find that it is not so difficult, but you did not know the game rules before. However, some projects do not need money to invest, because you can invest with other people's money. I didn't use my money before I invested in Airbnb. I used the bank's credit card. Some people would say that it was dangerous. If I failed, what would I do? Only a fool would do it and so on. I can only say to you: Ha ha, in fact, only you really understand the rules of the game, you can completely control the risk, why do you say so? Because before the project started, I had carefully studied the surrounding passenger flow situation, which is the age of tourists, how much passenger flow will be in each time period, and this is the city's largest tourist attraction, but there are almost no residential accommodation around, only a few small hotels. Secondly, as early as the time of signing the contract, it has been stated in the contract clause that if the tenant does not rent the house, I only need to compensate the landlord for one month's rent, and return the house to the landlord, while the decoration cost will be very low, which will reduce the risk. This practice is similar to the option payment in the United States. Easy to avoid risks and losses to the greatest extent. But the probability of profit is far greater than that of loss. As a result, the turnover increased sharply during the peak season. During this period, I only used the bank's money to invest. I didn't use my penny, but I made money again. Moreover, the rental policy on this side of China is to pay rent for four months at a time, (3 months rent and 1-month deposit). With only a small amount of money, we can get a good passive income. Finally, we deduct cleaning, utilities, and other expenses. The gross profit rate in the first year is 80%. I bought an Apple phone before, the price is 80%. The price is 4000 RMB, but although I am rich, I do not buy it in full, but in stages to the greatest extent. The longer the time is, the better it will be. I only need 160 RMB per month. Then, because a mobile game was very popular at that time, I bought two game accounts with 1000 RMB only and rented them on the game platform. The monthly income of a single account is the same. The benefit is 330 yuan, 2 accounts 660 yuan, with 660 yuan to return 160 yuan and 500 yuan more each month. What I want to say is that investing in your brain is always the right choice. In fact, opportunities are always around us, but you just don't have time to find them...

Does the decoration of the Airbnb cost a lot of money?

This problem is very expensive for people outside the industry. For hard-fitting, yes because it takes time and money to dismantle, but for soft-fitting, it saves money. In urban residential quarters, they are heavy on soft and light on hard-fitting, because hard-fitting transformation is a waste of time because, from the day you rent the house, there has been a cost every day. Soft-fitting high-speed decoration can be achieved in the shortest time, the most ideal effect can be the fastest start of business, recycling costs. Following is the price of tea sets, reclining chairs, telescopes, carpets, and wallpapers, plus other bedding, daily necessities and other total consumption will not exceed 1000 yuan, and 90 square meters of the house will certainly be completed within 7 days at the slowest, starting to quickly recycle the cost of funds, which is why I chose city Airbnb.

	直榜地中海创意木制鱼肯欢迎牌 海洋挂饰工艺品装饰 照片墙搭 配 【货品快照】 尺寸:鱼身30厘米 [交易保障]	7.00	1	**74.35** 含运费12.00
	实木雕发小鱼挂件地中海家居饰 品鱼串墙上装饰壁饰淘宝拍摄道 具大 【货品快照】 尺寸:中14cm*5.5cm*2cm [交易保障]	9.90	1	
	工艺 挂式泡沫救生圈 地中海风 格工艺品 家居装饰装饰救生圈 【货品快照】 尺寸:35cm蓝色 [交易保障]	13.00	1	
	7头青瓷鱼美釜鲤鱼杯茶具会销 礼品整套 陶瓷功夫茶具套装特 价批发 【货品快照】 颜色:单型蓝 [装搞3套][交易保障][7千包邮]	12.00	2	**29.76** 含运费11.00

		265.00	1		**280.00**
	天文望远镜单筒观暴看月亮学生入门级天文望远镜生日节日礼物礼品【货品快照】	85.00	1		**93.00**
	简约现代欧式客厅床边地垫茶几毯房间地毯卧室满铺可爱家用可机洗【货品快照】	45.00	1		**45.00**
	自粘墙纸防水纯色翻新贴纸卧室客厅温室店铺装饰墙纸灰色素色墙贴【货品快照】	2.50	25		**62.50**

Airbnb Automation Management

Airbnb belongs to the entity project, which is more stable than an Internet project. There are two modes to achieve passive income automation management.

The first is the trusteeship of the platform, such as domestic Tujia, Piggy, Freely have corresponding trusteeship policies, Tujia, Piggy are 3 and 7 Share Profits, you are responsible for providing decorated housing, the platform is responsible for operation and cleaning, day-to-day management. This model is suitable for new landlords, because, without experience, you may need someone else to help you with your day-to-day management. You can achieve passive income without doing anything. Every month you have money to enter into the account. Of course, the platform has certain conditions. The contract has been signed for at least two years. The policy of each platform is slightly different. Only when the decoration style of the house conforms to the relevant regulations of the platform can it be achieved. This platform （Freely）can even manage the house that has not been decorated. The platform is responsible for decorating your house and dealing with rental matters, but the contract period is also longer, generally more than five years. It is suitable for long-term rental houses, saving time and energy, and completely passive income. The second way is to take charge of the operation, receive the check-in order, send the check-in guide and room location to the tenants, because the room is fully automatic password lock, so the tenants can self-check-in, you only need to employ the cleaner in the platform after the tenants check-in, arrange cleaning to clean it, so you can also lie in the sofa at home. Make passive income. And these platforms have been opened in many countries around the world. If you want to join, you can easily earn a passive income.

Finally, I hope this book can help you, raise your horizon, earn more passive income and achieve financial freedom. If you like this book, please comment on Amazon. The author will continue to create more quality e-books. Thank you for your support.

THANK YOU!

My other book:

Passive Income-Your Automatic Money Making Machine

preview： Undoubtedly, we are now in the era and wave of the Internet. In the face of the pressure of life, rising prices and rising inflation, in addition to traditional investment channels (stocks, real estate, funds, etc.), what can be done? Defending our money, passive income, financial freedom is an ideal state of life, everyone wants to own, through this book you can understand that through the Internet you can also easily achieve passive income and achieve financial freedom.

https://www.amazon.com/dp/B07VL4QBXM